CH00375733

This book is to b[...]
the last date[...]

LOANS DIVISION,
275 KENNINGTON LANE
VAUXHALL   LONDON SE11 5QZ
TEL: 01-735 1338 – 01-735 7234

Longman Structural Readers:
Stage 2

Beowulf

Retold by Gordon Walsh

Illustrated by Michael Charlton

Longman

Longman Group Limited
London

*Associated companies, branches and representatives
throughout the world*

© Longman Group Ltd 1975

First published 1975
New impression 1977

ISBN 0 582 53804 1

Printed in Hong Kong by
Dai Nippon Printing Co. (H.K.) Ltd.

Some titles in this series:

1. Recommended for use with children (aged 8–12)
2. Recommended for use with young people (aged 12–15)
3. Recommended for use with older people (aged 15 plus)
   No figure: recommended for use with all ages

This story comes from a poem in Old English. The people in the poem lived here, 1400 years ago:

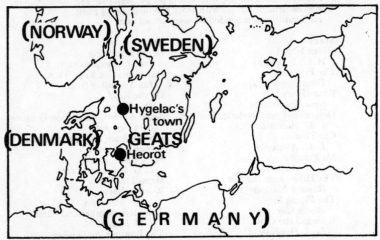

People from those lands went to England, and the poem went with them. 1200 years ago, a man in the north of England wrote the poem down.

Here are some lines from the old poem:

Ic mid élne scéall

góld gegángan,   oððe gúð nímeð

féorhbealu frécne   fréan éowerne!

("With my strength I shall get the gold, or an evil fight will take your old king!"—see page 35.) Each line has two "half-lines". The same first sounds come in each half-line, and each half-line has two stressed syllables. We have tried to write our poem like that. (Each line in our poem is a "half-line".)

The names are old, too. Their sounds are not like the English of today. We say them like this:

Beowulf [ˈbeəwulf]   *Hygelac* [ˈhygəlaːk]
Hrothgar [ˈhroːθgɑr]   *Weohstan* [ˈweəxstaːn]
Heorot [ˈheərot]   *Hrunting* [ˈhruntɪŋ]
Unferth [ˈunferθ]   *Wiglaf* [ˈwiːglɑːf]

BEOWULF

The soldiers are singing
   in the king's hall.
They are eating and drinking
   in the big room.
The king is there.
   His soldiers are with him.
The hall is happy.
   But over the fields,
Grendel waits.
   The monster is grim.
He hears the noise,
   but he is alone.

I

The monster is waiting
for the dark night.
He will go to the hall.

Now it is night.
The soldiers are sleeping.
Now it is quiet,
and Grendel can go.
Grimly, he moves
out of his den.
He walks alone
over the fields.
He comes to the hall.
The door stands open,
and Grendel moves

into the quiet room.

The men do not see him.
Angry and grim,
he stands alone.
He looks at the soldiers.
"Why can they be happy?"
the monster asks.
"I live alone.
I can't sing
with happy men.
The soldiers must die!"
Some men are sleeping
near the door.
Grendel goes
to the first man.

He takes the soldier   and kills him quickly.

He takes the soldier
in his strong arms,
    and kills him quickly.
His sleep will be long.
    The monster is gloating.
A second dies,
    and a third, and a fourth.
The monster kills
    thirty men
in his wicked work
    without a sound.
And grim Grendel
    stands and gloats.
Now those men
    will not drink or sing.
Quickly he goes
    to his dark den.
The soldiers' sleep
    is deep and quiet,
but the blood of their friends
    covers the walls.
And arms and heads,
    and legs and bodies,
cover the floor.
    The hall is red.

Morning comes.
    A soldier wakes.
Slowly, he sees
    the monster's work.
His shouts and cries
    wake his friends.

The king comes.
Sadly, he asks
"Which wicked
thing did this?
Did a monster
come to Heorot?"
A warrior speaks.
"There is a monster
in the dark woods.
He is wicked and strong.
His name is Grendel.
Now he knows Heorot,
and he will return."
That day,
the king and his warriors
clean the hall.
They burn the bodies
on a big fire.
Night comes,
and the tired men
sleep in the hall.
And Grendel returns.
The night is his time.
He takes some men,
and he drinks down
their warm blood.
He leaves quietly.
Morning comes,
and the soldiers see
their dead friends.
The fires burn
in their sad work.

They burn the bodies   on a big fire.

7

For twelve years,
   grim Grendel
visits Heorot.
   The hall is dark.
The warriors sleep
   in their little homes,
and the nights are quiet
   in the king's hall.

One day,
   a warrior is watching
the summer sea.
   A boat is coming.
Fifteen warriors
   with weapons and armour
jump to the land.
   The soldier meets them

with his sword in his hand.

"Stop!" he tells them.
"Why are you wearing
    armour here?
Do you want to fight us?"

"We don't want to fight,"
a warrior answers.

He is young and strong.
"My name is Beowulf.

We're Geats, and we're friends.
We're carrying weapons
    because we want to help you.
We want to fight
    your wicked monster."
The warrior laughs.

"I'll take you to the king,"
hc tells the Geats,

"but Grendel is strong
and your fight will be hard.
    He's already killed
hundreds of men
    in the dark nights."
They follow the soldier.
    In Heorot hall,
the warriors are working
    with their weapons and armour.
Hrothgar their king
    stops and looks.
Some men are coming,
    but he does not know them.
"My name is Beowulf,"
    a big man says.
"My uncle is Hygelac,
    the king of the Geats."
"Sit down, my friend,"
    old Hrothgar answers.
"I know your uncle.
    But why are you here?"
"You helped my father,"
    Beowulf tells him.
"Men tried to kill him,
    but you stood with him.
Now I'll help you.
    Can we stay in this hall
and fight your monster?"

    "You are young and strong,"
the king tells him.

    "Yes, you can stay;
but Grendel will give you

a hard fight."
So Beowulf's soldiers
   sit at the tables.
Night comes.
   The king and his men
go to their homes,
   and the Geats wait for Grendel.
"Take off your swords,"
   Beowulf says.
"Grendel doesn't
   have a sword,
so we'll fight with our hands."
   The men sleep.
Beowulf waits.
   Now Grendel comes.

He tries to crush   *that wicked creature.*

12

He breaks the door
  with his big arms.
He sees the warriors,
  and his face is grim.
For twelve years
  he has visited Heorot;
now men have returned.
  The warriors must die!
He takes the first
  and crushes his body.
He pulls off the arms,
  and drinks the blood.
Grendel is gloating.
  He drops the body
and comes to Beowulf.
  His bloody hands
touch the warrior.
  But Beowulf moves.
He jumps to his feet,
  and he takes the creature
in his strong arms.
  He tries to crush
that wicked creature,
  but Grendel is strong.
He fights hard.
  A table breaks.
Grendel and Beowulf
  drop to the floor.
The creature holds
  Beowulf's head.
His fingers find
  the warrior's eyes.

The noise of the fight
   wakes the soldiers,
and they move to Beowulf.
   "Stop!" he tells them.
"I'm going to kill
   this creature alone."
Suddenly he moves.
   He pushes hard
with his strong body.
   He jumps to his feet.
The monster waits.
   Beowulf turns.
His arms crush
   the creature again.
Grendel is tired.
   He cannot fight.
The Geat will kill him,
   Grendel knows.
He tries to run.
   But Beowulf is holding
his big arm.
   The monster moves,
and the arm breaks.
   With a loud cry,
Grendel runs
   from the grim warriors.
He leaves his arm
   in Beowulf's hands.
Black blood
   drops to the floor.
The warriors shout.
   Quickly, the king
comes with his men.

Hrothgar is happy.
Beowulf gives him
    Grendel's arm.
"Now you'll remember
    Beowulf and Grendel,"
he tells the king.
    "Yes, I'll remember,"
Hrothgar answers.
    He puts the arm
on the wall of Heorot.
    "Sleep now, my friend.
Your fight was hard,
    and you're very tired."
They clean the blood
    from the warrior's body.
Beowulf sleeps,

and Hrothgar's men
watch the hall.
Morning comes.
The warrior wakes
and goes outside.
There is black blood
from Grendel's body
over the fields.
"We'll follow the monster,"
a soldier says.
"The blood shows us
the way to his den.
We'll find it, and kill him."
They go over the fields,
but they do not find
Grendel's den
in the dark woods.
The blood takes them
to a black lake.
The water is deep,
and evil air
comes from it to the land.
"This place is evil,"
a soldier says.
"We can't stay here."
They watch the water,
but they do not see Grendel.
They leave the lake.
Night comes,
and the soldiers stay
in the king's hall.
Grendel has gone,
and they drink and sing.

But out in the lake
  a creature is moving.
Big and black,
  it comes from the water.
The moon lights
  its evil face.
Grimly, it comes
  over the fields
to Heorot hall.
  It is Grendel's mother!
Men killed her son;
  now she will kill them.
She walks to the hall
  and hears the noise.
The men can sing now—
  but they will die in the night.

17

mc

Big and black,   it comes from the water.

18

Beowulf and Hrothgar
leave the hall.
The trees are dark,
and the men do not see
the angry creature.
The noise stops.
The soldiers sleep.
Suddenly, the monster
breaks the door.
She goes into the hall.
Sadly, she sees
her son's arm
in the light of the moon.
She shouts, and the noise
wakes the warriors.
They grab their swords,
but the monster moves
very quickly.
She grabs the arm
and runs to the door.
An old soldier
is sleeping there.
She stops, and takes
the warrior too.
She leaves with his body
under her arm,
and runs into the night.
The warriors follow.
They look in the woods
and they go to the lake,
but they cannot find
their old friend.

19

They sadly return
  and tell their king.

It is morning, and Beowulf
  comes to the king.
Sad and grim,
  Hrothgar waits.
Beowulf stops.
  "What is it?" he asks.
He listens quietly.
  "I'll find your friend,"
he tells the king.
  He takes some soldiers.
They go to the lake,
  and there they stop.

They see the head
  of the old warrior
beside the water,
  but the body has gone.
The water is red
  with the warrior's blood.
"The monster lives
  at the bottom of the lake,"
a soldier says.
  "The body will be there."
The brave Weohstan
  is Beowulf's friend.
He goes to the lake.
  It is an evil place.
Wicked creatures
  are swimming in the water.

"I want to kill
    this monster," he says.
But Beowulf stops him.
    "No," he says.
"I killed her son,
    so she came to Heorot.
Wait here, Weohstan.
    I must kill
the monster's mother."
    He goes to the water.
Unferth calls to him.
    He is Hrothgar's man.
"You can take this sword.
    Its name is Hrunting,
and it's very old.
    It has taken the blood
of brave warriors.
    It will help you."
So Beowulf gives
    his sword to Weohstan.
With Hrunting in his hand,
    he goes into the lake.
He swims down
    in the black water,
and the dark creatures
    swim beside him.
Grendel's mother
    waits at the bottom.
The warrior cannot
    fight in the water.
He swims, and he finds
    the monster's den.

It is dry, with a fire.
  He leaves the water
and the monster follows.
  He swings his sword
at the creature's head,
  and hits it hard.
But Hrunting does not wound her.
  Angry, he drops it.
The creature grabs him
  and tries to crush him.
He drops to the ground,
  and she swings her knife
at Beowulf's body.
  But his armour is strong.
The knife cannot wound him.

23

He leaves the water   and the monster follows.

24

He jumps to his feet.
Suddenly, he sees
    a sword on the wall.
It is big and heavy,
    and very old.
He grabs it quickly
    and swings at the creature.
This weapon is strong.
    It wounds her badly.
She shouts, and stops;
    and slowly she dies.
Her black blood
    covers the floor.
Now Beowulf
    stands in her den,
and the fire shows him
    Grendel's body.

The dark face
    looks up from the floor.
The strong sword
    cuts off that head,
wicked and evil.
    He will take it to Hrothgar.
The lake is black
    with the monster's blood.
The warriors are waiting,
    and they watch it sadly.
"The monster's killed him,"
    Hrothgar says.
He leaves the lake.
    His men go with him,
but Beowulf's warriors
    watch and wait.

25

Down in the den,
   Beowulf finds
the creature's treasure.
   But he cannot carry it.
He is tired, so he takes
   the sword and the head
and returns to the water.
   He swims to his warriors.
They shout happily
   and they help him to the land.
Four men carry
   Grendel's head,
and two take
   the heavy sword.
They come to Heorot.

The king and his men
are talking sadly
about the warrior.
And brave Beowulf
comes into the hall.
The warriors run to him.
They laugh and shout.
Beowulf gives
the sword and the head
to happy Hrothgar.
That night,
Beowulf and Weohstan
drink with the king.
He gives Beowulf
gold and jewels.
The warrior has done
his brave work,
and the men can sleep
in Heorot hall.

Morning comes.
Now the Geats
must return to their land.
They leave Heorot
and go to their boat.
All the people
walk sadly
by the brave warriors.
And the Geats go
over the sea.
They come to their king.
Beowulf gives

Hrothgar's treasure
   to Hygelac the king.
And Hygelac gives
   land, and a hall,
and a big old sword
   to brave Beowulf.
He takes his men
   to the new hall.
Beowulf works
   and fights with his warriors,
and he gives them treasure.
   They live happily.

Suddenly, Hygelac
   dies in his hall.
He was Beowulf's uncle;

and now Beowulf
is king of the Geats.
　He is strong and kind,
and for fifty years
　he is a good king.

Weohstan dies,
　and Wiglaf, his son,
comes to the king.
　He lives in the hall.
From Beowulf's warriors,
　the young boy
learns to fight.
　And Beowulf loves him.

One night,
　a slave of the Geats
runs away
　from his angry master.
He is cold and tired.
　He sees the mouth
of a cave in a hill,
　and a light is burning.
The slave goes in.
　It is a treasure cave!
The slave sees
　gold and jewels,
weapons and armour.
　But near the mouth,
a dragon is sleeping.
　It watches the treasure.
Quietly, the man

29

moves in the cave
and goes to the gold.

The light dances
on a big cup.

It is heavy with jewels.
Softly, the slave
takes it, and runs.
He goes to his master
and gives him the cup.
The man is happy.

But morning comes.
The dragon wakes.

It loves that treasure.
Suddenly, it stops.

It stands and looks.
Where is the big
cup of gold?
Quickly, the creature
looks in its cave.
It moves the treasure.

It looks on the hill.
The cup has gone.

"A man has taken it,"
the dragon knows.

It waits in the cave,
alone and angry.

Night comes.
The dragon leaves.

In the light of the moon,
it follows the slave
and comes to the town.
It is breathing fire

from its angry mouth.
It breathes on the houses,
   and the town burns.
The people try
   to run away,
but men and women
   and children die.
The dragon comes
   to Beowulf's hall.
It breathes, and the hall
   burns in the fire.
Grimly, the dragon
   goes to its cave
and the soldiers bring
   the story to Beowulf.

It breathes on the houses, *and the town burns.*

"My people are dying.
  I must fight this dragon,"
the old king says.
  "I killed Grendel,
and the monster's mother.
  Give me my armour."
The men move,
  but Wiglaf stops them.
"Years ago,"
  he tells Beowulf,
"you killed those creatures.
  You're brave, and the king;
but I'm young and strong.
  I'll fight the dragon."
The old warrior
  looks at Wiglaf.
"No, my friend,"
  Beowulf says.
"I'm king of the Geats,
  and I must do it."
He tells his men:
  "Make a shield
of strong iron.
  My shield is wood,
and the fires will burn it."
  They give him the shield
with his weapons and armour.
  Eleven warriors
leave with the king.
  Wiglaf is one.
They are on their horses,
  but the slave and his master

come with the cup.
  "The creature wants this,"
the master says.
  He shows it to Beowulf.
The king says
  to the poor slave:
"You must show us the way
  to this treasure cave."
He wants to stay,
  but they give him a horse
and he must ride with the warriors.
  Near to the hill,
the slave shows them
  the mouth of the cave.
Beowulf says:
  "I'll kill this dragon
and get its gold,
  or an evil fight
will take your king."
  Bravely, he walks
to the mouth of the cave.
  He sees the fire.
He stops, and gives
  a loud shout.
The dragon hears
  the voice of a man.
Quickly, it comes.
  It sees the king
and it breathes fire.
  Beowulf stands.
The dragon flies at him.
  Its hot fire

Beowulf stands.   *The dragon flies at him.*

burns the shield.

Beowulf fights,
but the creature is strong.

He cannot stop it.
The king's clothes
burn in the fire.
The fight is hard.

He is going to die.
His soldiers see this,
and they run from the fight.
But Wiglaf stays.

He shouts to the warriors:
"You wicked men!

Why are you running?
The king's given us
gold and jewels,
swords and shields.

We must stay and help him!"
But the men ride
quickly away.
They leave the warriors.

Wiglaf goes
alone to his king,
and stops the fire.
The dragon comes.

Its fire burns
Wiglaf's shield.

Beowulf sees
the creature's head,
and he hits it hard.
The sword breaks,
but he has hit the creature.

It swings its foot   *and wounds him badly.*

38

The dragon is angry.
  It swings its foot
at Beowulf's head
  and wounds him badly.
The king's blood
  runs to the ground.
Angrily, Wiglaf
  swings his sword.
He hits the dragon
  under the head
and the weapon makes
  a deep wound.
The fire stops.
  Beowulf is dying,
but he stands on his feet
  and takes his knife.
The two warriors
  kill the monster.

Old Beowulf
  tries to breathe,
but his life is going.
  He drops to the ground.
"I'm dying, Wiglaf,"
  he says slowly.
"You're young and brave.
  You stayed and helped me."
He gives Wiglaf
  his king's collar.
"Now, son of Weohstan,
  you must be king of the Geats.
I must follow your father."

39

The two warriors   kill the monster.

And Beowulf dies.
Wiglaf sadly
   looks on the ground
at Beowulf's body.
   The brave warrior
has killed the creature,
   but the king has died.
He takes the body
   in his strong arms
and cries alone
   for his king and friend.

Wiglaf is king.

On the hill, his soldiers
build a fire
for the warrior's body.
The men on the sea,
and the people in the towns,
will see the fire.

They will remember Beowulf.

Exercises in Comprehension and Structure

1. Look at this sentence:

   The men see Grendel.

   We can change this. We can say:

   The men *do not see* Grendel.

   Change these sentences too:

   1. The Geats want to fight Hrothgar's men.
   2. Hrothgar knows Beowulf and his men.
   3. Grendel has a sword.
   4. Beowulf can carry the monster's treasure.
   5. "Help me!"
   6. Grendel will return to Heorot.

2. Write these sentences with the right form of the verb:

   1. The soldiers ——— (sleep) now.
   2. Grendel ——— (hear) the noise.
   3. The monster ——— already ——— (kill) hundreds of men.
   4. The soldiers cannot find Grendel's mother. She——— (go).
   5. Beowulf killed Grendel, so his mother ——— (come) to Heorot.
   6. "A man ——— (take) the cup," the dragon knows.

3. Write these sentences with **can** or **must**:

   1. "The man ——— die," says Grendel's mother.
   2. Men ——— not live in the evil lake.
   3. Grendel has gone; the soldiers ——— live in Heorot.
   4. The soldiers look for the old man, but they ——— not find him.
   5. Beowulf says, "I ——— kill the monster."
   6. Grendel is wicked. He ——— not live.

4. Write these sentences with **to** or **at**:

   1. Grendel's mother listens ——— the noise.
   2. She runs ——— the door.
   3. She swings her knife ——— Beowulf's body.
   4. Beowulf and Hrothgar sit ——— the table.
   5. The dragon goes ——— the town.

5. Look at these sentences:

I'm going to fight the dragon.
Beowulf is going to die.

We can say:

I'll fight the dragon.
Beowulf will die.

Write these sentences with **will** or **'ll**:

1. Grendel is going to return.
2. I'm going to help you.
3. We're going to fight with our hands.
4. The soldiers are going to die in the night.
5. Beowulf is going to take the head to Hrothgar.
6. The people are going to remember Beowulf.

6. Look at these sentences:

a) Hygelac dies (sudden).   b) He is (old).

We must say:

a) Hygelac dies sudden*ly*.   b) He is *old*.

Write these sentences as a) or b):

1. The monster moves (quick).
2. Grendel leaves (quiet).
3. The cup is (heavy) with jewels.
4. Beowulf hits the dragon's head (hard).
5. The old sword wounds the creature (bad).